NAVIGATING THE LIBRARY

VALERIE BODDEN | ILLUSTRATIONS BY ELWOOD H. SMITH

CREATIVE ⬤ EDUCATION

Published by Creative Education
P.O. Box 227, Mankato, Minnesota 56002
Creative Education is an imprint of The Creative Company
www.thecreativecompany.us

Design and production by Liddy Walseth
Art direction by Rita Marshall
Printed in the United States of America

Illustrations by Elwood H. Smith © 2012

Library of Congress Cataloging-in-Publication Data

Bodden, Valerie.
Navigating the library / by Valerie Bodden.
p. cm. — (Research for writing)
Includes bibliographical references and index.
Summary: A narrative guide to conducting research at the library,
complete with an overview of methodologies, tips for finding materials
in databases and on the shelves, and helpful resources.
ISBN 978-1-60818-206-0
1. Library research—Juvenile literature. 2. Research—Methodology—
Juvenile literature. 3. Information resources—Juvenile literature.
4. Information literacy—Juvenile literature. 5. Libraries—Juvenile literature. I. Title.

Z710.B63 2012
020.72—dc23   2011040492

CPSIA: 021413 PO1656
2 4 6 8 9 7 5 3

TABLE OF CONTENTS

YOU CONDUCT RESEARCH EVERY DAY.
AND YOU PROBABLY DON'T EVEN REALIZE IT.

When you want to know the score of last night's football game, you check on-line. If you're wondering how to spell (or define) "supercilious," you get out the dictionary. And when you've forgotten the math assignment, you e-mail your friends to ask them. Although these research situations are rather informal, the skills you use for them are similar to those you need to conduct research for writing. After all, research is basically just a search—a search for sources that contain specific, **relevant**, and accurate information about your topic.

At some point during nearly every research project, you will find yourself in need of a library. Why? Libraries contain information that you can't get any-where else—and that information is organized in a way that makes it easy to complete a **systematic** search. Say, for example, that you want to research Mt. Everest. The library can provide you with **autobiographies** by the first men to ever reach the summit, videos of the Himalayas, and even online journal articles about scientific studies that have been done on the mountain.

Although every library is unique, most libraries follow similar systems for organizing their items, cataloging their holdings, and lending materials to patrons. In addition, nearly every library features one indispensable resource—the reference librarian, who can help you in your quest for information. So the next time you need to look something up, make the library one of your first stops. It will likely have what you need—and then some!

LOOKING
TO THE
LIBRARY

WITH SO MUCH INFORMATION AVAILABLE ON THE INTERNET TODAY, it may seem like a waste of time to visit the library. Aren't those places just for people who don't know how to use computers? Actually, no. Libraries are useful for almost everyone. The works on a library's shelves represent more than 2,000 years' worth of information—and many of the particular resources in which that information can be found are not available online. Only a small percentage of books can be accessed online, for example, and journal articles often appear only in print or through a library's online subscription. Sure, a library search may take a bit more time than simply googling a few terms—but the results will also likely be more relevant and more reliable. And it's not as if library research doesn't involve computers. In fact, the majority of libraries use online book catalogs and subscribe to a number of online journals. In most cases, you can even access these resources from a computer outside the library.

Today, there are more than 122,000 libraries in the United States. The vast majority—about 99,000—are school libraries; another 9,000 are public libraries; and the remainder are academic (at universities), government, and special libraries (belonging to companies or dedicated to a specific field such as medicine or law). In addition, there is one national library— the Library of Congress in Washington, D.C.—that collects copies of as much of the literature produced in the country as possible, along with many international works.

Help, please.

FIGURE OUT EXACTLY WHAT YOU NEED

Although the Library of Congress is the largest library in the world, you probably won't travel there for your research projects. When you are looking for information, you will most likely head to your school library, which contains materials that have been selected by librarians because they think the information within them will be useful to students. Or you might use the public library, which serves members of the general public and may have information on topics not covered by the works in your school library. Academic libraries generally have more in-depth information on scholarly topics, in addition to the regular fiction and nonfiction titles popular in other libraries.

The keys to conducting effective library research are knowing what you are looking for, where to find it, and how to evaluate it. These skills are known as information literacy, and according to the American Library Association, a person who has mastered them has "learned how to learn." The first step in becoming information literate—and in conducting research in the library or anywhere else—may seem obvious, but having a specific plan is more complicated than it at first appears. For example, if you enter your library with the idea of researching World War II, you will be quickly overwhelmed. Your library may have hundreds of resources on that subject—and you can't possibly read them all. Just browsing through them to determine which might be the most useful could take a few hours! In this case, you must narrow your search. Ask yourself what aspect of World War II you want to dig into. Perhaps it's a specific battle, treatment of prisoners of war, the atomic bomb, or life on the American home front. Or maybe you aren't sure

what it is that you want to know about the war. That's okay, too—you can still make use of the library. Just head to the reference department and pick up an encyclopedia. Reading the World War II entry may help you zero in on a specific area of interest.

Perhaps, after some careful thought and background reading, you decide that you'd like to focus on the role of women in World War II. You can continue on your quest to becoming information literate by identifying the keywords that will aid in your search. "Women" and "World War II"

ESTABLISH THE CREDIBILITY

are obvious choices. But you might also consider searching **synonyms** and related terms. For example, from your background reading you may know that many women served as nurses in the war and that others went to work on the home front. So you could add "nursing" and

"employment" to your list of terms. Generating such a list—and keeping track of which terms yield successful results—will make for an easier search.

Once you've completed that search and have your information in hand, the hard work is done, right? Not so fast! An important part of information literacy is evaluating the quality of what you have found. Although the materials in a library have been carefully selected by librarians, they may not all contain equally credible (or the most updated) information. To establish the credibility of a source found in the library, first consider the author. Is she an expert in the field? Many books contain an author **biography** with information about the author's credentials and expertise. You can also look the author up on the Internet for further information.

For the most part, libraries provide books and other works produced by reputable publishers, but you should still look into a source's publication information, too. If a book was published by an academic press (such as Harvard University Press), it is likely reliable, especially since many academic publishers require their books to be reviewed by a panel of experts in the field before being published. The same is true of many academic journals. Look at the publication date as well. Is the information current? This may be more important for some subjects (computers, technology, or medicine, for example) than for others (such as literary analysis or history).

In evaluating a source's reliability, you can also look beyond the author and publication information to the content itself. Does the information provided match that of other sources? If there are inconsistencies, is there a reason for them? (Is this new data, for example, or a new way of looking at an old problem?) Does the author **cite** sources to back up her claims? Don't be afraid to check those sources and to also spot-check the figures in one source against those in another—after all, you're at the library, and sources abound! As you think about a source's reliability, consider also the possibility that an author may be **biased**. Does she seem to support a specific point of view? Such bias is not wrong—in fact, we all have some biases, since we all have opinions. But you need to be aware of an author's bias in order to properly interpret the information she provides.

Once you have found a credible source, you also need to determine whether it is relevant to your topic. Even the most reputable source won't do you any good if it doesn't have anything to do with your subject. For example, if you are researching Michael Jordan's basketball career, sources about his time playing professional baseball probably won't be much help (unless you want to compare his experiences in the two sports). You can skim a book's introduction or glance through its **index** to determine whether it might be helpful. For articles, check out the beginnings of each section or read an abstract, or summary, of the work to help you decide whether to use it.

Finally, once you have found the information you need, be sure to use it responsibly. Keep track of the author, title, and publication information for every source (either in a computer file or on index cards), and if you use an idea that isn't your own, be sure to cite where it originated. Likewise, if you use someone else's words directly, put them in quotation marks. By the time you've finished writing, you'll wonder what you would have done without the library and all the resources it provides!

A HISTORY OF INFORMATION-KEEPING

Libraries have been important locations for storing information for more than 4,000 years. The first libraries were basically record rooms or archives, used to store clay tablets containing the public records of the Babylonians and other early civilizations. In ancient Greece, libraries were kept in a number of temples, and larger libraries began to be formed around the 4th century B.C. to hold philosophical writings and scientific research. During the Middle Ages, university libraries began to be established in a number of European cities, while private collectors set up their own libraries during the Renaissance. By the 19th century, a new emphasis was placed on the organization and cataloging of books, and some governments began to provide public libraries to their citizens. The library was revolutionized in the late 20th century, as computer systems allowed a library's collection to be accessed remotely through online catalogs and databases.

GETTING ORIENTED

IF YOU'VE NEVER REALLY TAKEN A GOOD LOOK AROUND YOUR LIBRARY— or if you're visiting a new library for the first time—you might feel a bit overwhelmed. Shelves of books, racks of magazines and journal articles, banks of computers—what if you get lost? Some libraries offer guided tours—you can check at the information desk to find out if yours does. But even if it doesn't, you can give yourself a tour. Just walking around and looking at shelves and signs can give you a pretty good idea of where everything is.

Although every library is arranged slightly differently, most share several common features. For example, fiction books (containing imagined, rather than real-life, stories) and nonfiction (factual) books are usually shelved separately. In addition, most libraries have separate areas for newspapers and magazines, audiovisual materials such as CDs and DVDs, and reference collections. Within or near the reference section, you will also likely find the reference desk, where you can ask a professional librarian for assistance with your research if needed. And near the door, you will probably see the circulation desk, where you can check out books.

Many of a modern library's resources are online, so be sure to give yourself a tour of the library's Web site as well. Click around to learn about library policies (such as how many books or DVDs you can check out at a time), to find the library's online catalog, and to discover the online databases to which your library provides access. You can either tour the Web site from a library computer or from a computer outside the building.

Once you have a feel for where everything is in the library, you can figure out where to concentrate your search. You may make use of just one type of a library's resources—or maybe you'll need a little bit of everything. When you think of a library, you probably think of books. And the bulk of a library's physical space is usually taken up by books. You can browse the shelves to find one that looks interesting or, if you are looking for information on a specific topic, you can check the library's catalog to find out which books are available and where to find them within the library's collection. Books are useful for research on almost any topic; although, because of the time

required to publish a book, they may not have the most up-to-date information on a subject. Most libraries allow you to check out books for a period ranging from one week to one month. All you need is a library card. If you don't already have one, get one—it's usually free to local residents (although you may need a parent with you to sign for the card if you're **ALL YOU NEED IS A LIBRARY CARD** under a certain age), and it will give you access to just about anything you need in the library.

Most libraries also have a periodicals section, where you can find items such as newspapers, magazines, and journals. Because they are usually published daily, weekly, monthly, or quarterly, these sources often provide the latest information available on a subject. Newspapers are especially useful for local or **controversial** subjects; general interest magazines can provide an overview and interpretation of current topics; and scholarly journals, aimed at an audience of experts, contain the latest studies and findings in a field. Generally, the most recent issues of a periodical are kept on the shelf (usually arranged by category or alphabetically by title) and can often be checked out, although the current issue may have to remain in the library. You may be able to search your library's catalog for periodicals; or you can rely on a print index such as *Readers' Guide to Periodical Literature* (usually found in the reference section), which provides a listing of articles

in more than 300 popular periodicals, arranged by subject and author. You can also check your library's online periodical databases, which may provide publication information, abstracts, or links to the full text of articles.

While some online databases provide access to articles dating back to the 19th century from major newspapers such as *The New York Times*, for old copies of the local newspaper, you will probably have to check out your library's microfilm, or microfiche, collection. These small rolls of film, which contain tiny photographs of a newspaper's pages, can be read only with a microfilm reader, a machine that magnifies the images on a screen. Microfilm is often kept in a separate section of the library, sometimes near the reference section or the periodical collection. For help in finding specific microfilm reels or in learning how to use a microfilm reader, check with a librarian.

The reference section is among the most powerful areas of the library for conducting research, especially when you are just beginning your hunt. Reference works such as encyclopedias can give you a general overview of your topic and help you to identify a specific aspect that interests you. They can also clue you in to keywords and special terminology. For many subjects, specialized encyclopedias and dictionaries are also available. For example, *The Grove Dictionary of Art* contains entries on art terminology, artistic movements, and artists. Both general and specialized encyclopedias can lead you to further resources, as articles typically include a **bibliography**.

To find an even longer list of potential sources for your subject, you can consult one of the reference section's book-length bibliographies or indexes. These works provide lists of the books and articles published on specific subjects in major fields. If you are researching the history of the World Series, for example, you might look for a copy of *The Baseball Bibliography*, which lists thousands of published works about baseball, including specific references to works about the World Series. Many bibliographies and indexes are also annotated, meaning they provide a brief description or summary of the works listed. Although they won't tell you where to find a book or article—or even whether your library owns a copy—bibliographies are a great place to find out what has already

BIBLIOGRAPHIES
KEYWORDS
been written about your topic. And once you

know that, you can try to track down the sources you need.

In addition to encyclopedias and bibliographies, most reference sections also include atlases, handbooks, and fact books such as almanacs. Keep in mind, though, that you'll have to peruse any reference works while you're at the library, as they are usually non-circulating—which means they can't be checked out. Some of the items in the reference department may also be available online through your library's database, but many are found only in print.

The reference sections of some libraries also contain government documents and publications. At other libraries, these records may be kept in a separate department or may be shelved with the nonfiction collection. If you are looking for information about public policy or law, you might check with your librarian to find out exactly where and how to locate government records, since some libraries do not include them in their online catalogs.

Although most of what you find in a library is in print, nearly every library also provides access to non-print resources such as CDs and DVDs. If you are researching a particular movie, actor, or director, for example, you might find a DVD useful. Don't overlook your library's audiovisual collection for other topics as well. Many of the DVDs in a library are documentary or educational in nature and can be useful for researching everything from George Washington to Paris Hilton and from the War of 1812 to the War in Afghanistan. In addition, CDs may contain audiobooks related to your subject. So the next time you go to the library, take a good look around— you will find information everywhere!

CHECK WITH YOUR LIBRARIAN

SELF-GUIDED TOUR

The best way to learn what your library has and where it is kept is to give yourself a tour. So make a visit to either your school library or the local public library and take a walk around. Make note of where the circulation desk is, where fiction and nonfiction titles are shelved, and where you can find periodicals and audiovisual materials. Then find your library's reference department and take a moment to browse the shelves. What kinds of reference works does your library provide? Also look for computers that you can use for database searching. Take a few minutes to click through your library's Web site to find which databases are offered. Before you leave, you might talk to a librarian about any special collections housed in your library. And don't forget to sign up for a library card, if you don't already have one!

ORGANIZATION AND MORE ORGANIZATION

YOU ALREADY KNOW THAT THE ITEMS IN A LIBRARY ARE ORGANIZED
according to type—nonfiction books in one area, fiction books in another,
reference books in still another, not to mention audiovisual materials and
periodicals in their own sections. But even if you know that you are looking
for a particular book or magazine, how do you go about finding it? After all,
locating one book among your library's vast collection, which may number
in the hundreds of thousands or even in the millions, could take years!
Fortunately, libraries do more than sort their items by type; they also classify
and organize their collections, assigning each item a **call number** and placing
it on the shelf in a specific order to make it easy to find.

Call numbers are not random assortments of numbers and letters
designed to confuse researchers like you. In fact, understanding call
numbers can make it easier to find the resources you need—and even tell
you something about them. In most libraries, works of fiction are arranged
alphabetically by the author's last name. So if you find a call number that
consists of all letters, you are likely looking at a
novel, short story collection, or other fictional
work. For nonfiction, the majority of libraries
assign call numbers using one of two systems:
the Dewey Decimal system or the Library
of Congress system. In general, elementary
school, middle school, high school, and public
libraries use the Dewey Decimal system, while

university and other academic libraries usually classify their works according to the Library of Congress system. In both systems, materials are assigned a combination of numbers and/or letters based on their subject, or classification.

The Dewey Decimal system divides all works into 10 general subject areas, each designated by a 3-digit number. Works on religion, for example, fall into the 200s category, while works on history are classified in the 900s. Each broad category is further broken down into 10 sections—the 930s represent works on ancient history, for example—and then these sections are each broken down into 10 more subcategories. So, within ancient history, you can find works on ancient Egypt (932), ancient Greece (938), and other ancient cultures. In some cases, the three-digit number is followed by a decimal point and additional numbers, which further define the subject. If there are a number of books on the same subject, the second line of the call number assigns letters or a series of letters and numbers to each book, usually based on the author's last name.

In contrast, the Library of Congress system separates books into 21 subject classes, which are based on a classification system set up by the Library of Congress in the late 1800s to organize its own collection. Each subject class is assigned its own letter, and in many cases, the subject area is further broken down by the addition of a second letter. In this system, works on world history are assigned the letter D, while DT is used for books about the history of Africa. The call number continues with up to four numbers and sometimes a decimal point followed by additional numbers and letters. Works on Egyptian history, for example, are assigned a call number falling somewhere between DT43 and DT154, depending on the specific aspect of Egypt covered, such as its pyramids or peoples.

Knowing the general subject categories for the Dewey Decimal and Library of Congress systems can lead you to the right section of the library for your search. For example, if you are researching ancient Egypt, you now know to look in the 932s using the Dewey system or the DT43–154s using the Library of Congress system. But depending on how extensive your library's collection of books on the subject is, it might take you a long time to locate a relevant work that way. Additionally, even among libraries that use the same systems, the call number assigned a particular work can vary slightly from one library to the next. Some public libraries may assign a book about Egyptian pyramids a Dewey number of 932, for example, while others may place the book in the 690s, the subject area classification for works about buildings. So it pays to find the specific call number of the works you need before you search the shelves. And that's

AUTHOR TITLE SUBJECT KEYWORD

where your library's catalog comes in.

Today, most libraries have online catalogs that can be used either in the library or remotely. Most catalogs allow you to search a library's holdings by author, title, subject, or keyword. Although they may sound similar, there is a difference between a subject search and a keyword search. A keyword search looks for your search terms anywhere within a record, including the title, author name, subject heading, or even the item's description, if there is one. A subject search, on the other hand, searches only the subject headings of each record. Many libraries use standardized subject headings, often based on a document called the *Library of Congress Subject Headings*. Unfortunately, these subject headings are not always obvious to those who don't categorize information for a living. If you are researching Americans' Constitutional rights, for example, you will find information under the subject heading civil rights. Fortunately, some catalogs provide suggested subjects if the terms you enter do not match their subject headings exactly. To track down the specific subject heading you need, you can check out the *Library of Congress Subject Headings* in print (usually held in the library's reference section) or online (id.loc.gov/authorities/subjects.html).

Some library catalogs also allow you to narrow your search by format (book, DVD, magazine), reading level (juvenile or adult), or date published.

You may also be able to do a **Boolean** search, in which you specify combinations of words that should be included or excluded from your keyword search. For example, using the search terms "Disney and movies not theme parks" should return results about Disney movies while eliminating those having to do with Disney World and other Disney parks.

It may take a few different word combinations, but eventually your search of the catalog is likely to produce useful results. When it does, make note of the location (reference, periodicals, nonfiction) of the works, as well as their call numbers. Then go and grab the resources you need. Since nonfiction books are shelved in numerical order based on their call numbers, this

should be an easy task. Each shelf is labeled to indicate which call numbers are housed there (for example 001–122), so just follow the signs until you find the shelf you need—and then follow the call numbers printed on the spines of the books until you get to the one you want. While you're there, it doesn't hurt to glance at the books surrounding it. Perhaps there is a useful one that you didn't come across in your search of the catalog.

The library catalog is only one useful electronic tool offered by your library, though. Don't overlook the many other research resources your library may provide online, including encyclopedias and periodical databases. Among the more common online databases are OCLC First Search, EBSCO Academic Search Premier, LexisNexis Academic, and ProQuest Newsstand. A number of libraries

GO AND GRAB THE RESOURCES YOU NEED

have also begun to offer access to e-books through their own collections or through services such as NetLibrary. Searching library databases is similar to searching the catalog. Most services allow you to search by keyword, author, title, or subject, and many also allow you to limit your search to specific publications or dates or to use Boolean operators. So whether you start your search in the library building or on the library Web site, remember that the information you are looking for has been organized—and that you can use that organization to find the sources you need!

DIVIDING KNOWLEDGE

In a library, all the world's knowledge is divided into categories, and knowing those categories can help you find the works you are looking for. The Dewey Decimal system includes 10 broad categories: computers, information, and general reference (000); philosophy and psychology (100); religion (200); social sciences (300); language (400); natural sciences and mathematics (500); technology (600); the arts (700); literature (800); and geography and history (900). The Library of Congress system, on the other hand, separates information into 21 classes: general works (A); philosophy, psychology, and religion (B); auxiliary sciences of history (such as archaeology or genealogy) (C); world history (D); American history (E); local American history (F); geography, anthropology, and recreation (G); social sciences (H); political science (J); law (K); education (L); music (M); fine arts (N); language and literature (P); science (Q); medicine (R); agriculture (S); technology (T); military science (U); naval science (V); and bibliography and library science (Z).

THE HUMAN TOUCH

ALTHOUGH THE ABILITY TO SEARCH THE LIBRARY CATALOG ELECTRONICALLY

and to sort through journal articles online has made using the library easier and more convenient, sometimes you still need a real live person to help with your research questions. This is where the reference librarian comes in. You can often find at least one reference librarian stationed near the reference collection, while others may be located throughout the building in a larger library. A reference librarian is an expert in research and the organization of information (and often in at least one other subject area as well). It is his job to help you find the information you need—no matter how obscure it may be. Unlike a computer, a reference librarian can ask you questions about what you need, what you've searched for, and what you've already found—and he can apply critical thinking skills to help you solve your research problem.

Most reference librarians can help with almost every aspect of your research project, from teaching you how to use the library's online catalog to helping you determine search terms and locate hard-to-find resources. When you are talking to a reference librarian, it is helpful to make your questions as specific as possible. For example, if you tell the librarian that you are looking for information on pollution, he may direct you to works on air pollution rather than to resources on water pollution or the history of waste or the environmental movement. Fortunately, even if you do ask a general question, most librarians are trained to interview you, asking questions to find out exactly what it is you are looking for. And if you aren't sure what that is (maybe you didn't realize there were so many topics related to pollution, for instance), he can help you narrow that down, too.

Maybe after talking to the librarian, you decide that what you really want information about is environmental law. Now that he knows exactly what you are looking for, the librarian may direct you to search the online catalog for the subjects "environmental law" or "environmental law, international" or "environmental law—cases" or even "environmental education—law and legislation." He may also help you identify periodical databases that contain relevant sources, including scientific journals and newspaper articles about newly passed environmental laws. He may even be able to direct you to a specialized encyclopedia or to government documents regarding environmental law.

24 HOURS A DAY, 7 DAYS A WEEK

Just a couple of decades ago, the only way to solicit help from a reference librarian was to talk to him in person at the library or on the phone. Although these methods are still perfectly acceptable—and often used—ways to get help, reference librarians are now available online as

well, often 24 hours a day, 7 days a week. Many library Web sites provide a link to their reference librarian's e-mail address or supply a Web form to submit questions to a librarian. The librarian receives the questions and then responds (usually via e-mail) anywhere from a few minutes to a few days later.

Whenever you need to e-mail your librarian or fill out a Web form, be sure to provide as much information as possible, including what, specifically, you need, its purpose (he may provide different sources if you are planning a trip to Colorado than if you are writing a report on the state for school, for example), and where you have already looked. That way, the librarian will not have to come back to you with further questions, which would add to the response time. If you need a more immediate answer to your question, you might look for a link that allows you to chat with or send an instant message to a reference librarian. In this case, you are communicating with your librarian in real time, so he can ask you questions and provide information right then and there. A growing number of libraries also accept reference questions sent by text message and will send a return text to the patron's phone.

In addition to answering your questions, reference librarians can help you obtain resources that are not owned by their library. Most libraries provide a service known as interlibrary loan, through which they can request books from other libraries around the state or country, or sometimes even from around the world.

Many libraries are part of a local association, or system, with other libraries in the same geographic region or of the same type. Their catalogs often include not only their own holdings but also the holdings of the other libraries in the system, which patrons can request and have delivered to their home library, often with a simple click of a button.

Sometimes, though, you may find that neither your home library nor the other libraries in the system have all the resources you need. In that case, you might check a statewide catalog—ask your librarian if your state provides one online—or an international catalog such as WorldCat (www.worldcat .org). You can also check the Library of Congress online catalog (catalog.loc .gov), which contains 14 million records, ranging from books and periodicals to computer files and sound recordings. If you find an item you need in one of these catalogs, bring the publication information (including author, title, publisher, and date) to your librarian. You don't need to know which library holds the information; your librarian will figure that out and submit an interlibrary loan request to that library. Or, with some libraries, you can make your own request online.

MAKE YOUR OWN REQUEST

Your librarian might not be able to obtain every item you request, depending on the policies of the libraries that hold the materials, but he will try his best. Be aware, though, that the interlibrary loan process can take a week or more, so be sure to make your request early. In addition, some libraries may charge a small fee for interlibrary loan services or may limit the number of interlibrary loan items you can request at one time. Once an interlibrary loan book arrives at your library, you will usually be allowed to check it out for a specified period of time. When you are done, you can return it to your home library, and the librarians will see that it gets back to the lending library. If your request is for a journal or magazine article, you will probably be given a print or electronic copy of the article that you can keep.

As you get to know more about your library, you may find that it offers other services as well, including classes in research skills, online searching,

PUT THAT INFORMATION TO USE!

or how to make the most of library resources.

There are probably also computers available for accessing the Internet or using basic word processing software. You can usually sign up to use one of these at the reference or circulation desk. In addition, many libraries house special collections of photographs, artwork, maps, postcards, music, manuscripts, or **artifacts** relating to a number of topics, such as local history. These items may be kept in a separate area of the library, and they may not be included in the catalog, so if your library has a special collection that might prove useful, be sure to talk to your reference librarian about how to access it.

From human librarians to computerized catalogs, libraries have all kinds of tools to help you find the information you need. And since that information is logically organized, you don't have to spend your time wandering (or clicking) aimlessly. Instead, you can figure out what you need and where to find it. Then it's up to you to put that information to use!

USING WHAT YOU KNOW

Put your library skills to the test by conducting a practice search. First, pick a topic that interests you, then head to the library. One of the first places you might want to check out is the reference section. Once you have used reference works to gain a general understanding of your topic, search your library's catalog for nonfiction books. Choose a few that look relevant and note their call numbers. Now see if you can find them on the shelves. Don't forget to search the library's online databases as well, either from the library or from an outside computer. Can you find any full-text articles on your subject? For articles that do not provide the full text, check to see if your library owns a print copy of the periodical in which it appears. When you have completed your search, evaluate your sources—do they appear to be relevant and reliable?

GLOSSARY

anthropology—the study of human culture and development

archives—collections of documents or items of historical importance, or the buildings (or online locations) where such documents or items are stored

artifacts—objects made by humans (as opposed to naturally occurring objects)

autobiographies—stories of a person's life, written by the person him- or herself

auxiliary—providing help or support, as in auxiliary sciences of history, which are scientific disciplines such as archaeology that help researchers evaluate and understand historical sources

biased—having a preference for or dislike of a certain person or idea that prevents one from making impartial judgments of that person or idea

bibliography—a list of books used in the preparation of a book or article or of books on a specific subject or by a specific author, along with publication information (author, title, publisher, date) for each

biography—the history of a person's life, written by someone other than that person

Boolean—a system of logic that combines the words "and," "or," and "not" to establish relationships between terms and ideas

call number—a series of numbers and letters assigned to a book to indicate its position on a library's shelves

cite—to quote someone else's work as evidence for an idea or argument

controversial—causing or marked by disagreements and arguments

databases—organized collections of data, or information, stored on a computer

genealogy—the study of family history

index—in the context of books and articles, a catalog or list of specific items, often arranged alphabetically and providing details about where to find them

Middle Ages—the period of European history lasting from about the 5th century through the 14th century A.D.

psychology—the study of the mind and behavior

relevant—related or connected to the idea or topic being discussed

Renaissance—the period of European history, from about the 14th through 17th centuries, marked by a renewal of art and literature and the beginnings of modern science and exploration

synonyms—words that have the same (or nearly the same) meaning

systematic—done in an organized way

WEB SITES

"Do We" Really Know Dewey?
http://library.thinkquest.org/5002/
Learn more about the Dewey Decimal system through this site composed by sixth-graders.

Learning to Research in the Library
http://www.ipl.org/div/aplus/library.htm
Check out tips for library research, as provided by the Internet Public Library.

Library of Congress Bibliographies, Research Guides, and Finding Aids
http://www.loc.gov/rr/program/bib/bibhome.html
Browse the multitude of research topics for which the Library of Congress provides detailed bibliographies.

The Seven Steps of the Research Process
http://olinuris.library.cornell.edu/ref/research/skill1.htm
Review the critical steps involved in research with this outline created by the Cornell University Library.

SELECTED BIBLIOGRAPHY

Anson, Chris M., Robert A. Schwegler, and Marcia F. Muth. *The Longman Writer's Bible: The Complete Guide to Writing, Research, and Grammar.* New York: Pearson Longman, 2006.

Ballenger, Bruce. *The Curious Researcher: A Guide to Writing Research Papers.* New York: Pearson Longman, 2004.

Booth, Wayne C., Gregory G. Colomb, and Joseph M. Williams. *The Craft of Research.* Chicago: University of Chicago Press, 2008.

George, Mary W. *The Elements of Library Research: What Every Student Needs to Know.* Princeton: Princeton University Press, 2008.

Lane, Nancy, Margaret Chisholm, and Carolyn Mateer. *Techniques for Student Research: A Comprehensive Guide to Using the Library.* New York: Neal-Schuman Publishers, 2000.

MLA Handbook for Writers of Research Papers. New York: The Modern Language Association of America, 2009.

Rodrigues, Dawn, and Raymond J. Rodrigues. *The Research Paper: A Guide to Library and Internet Research.* Upper Saddle River, N.J.: Prentice Hall, 2003.

Toronto Public Library. *The Research Virtuoso: Brilliant Methods for Normal Brains.* Toronto: Annick Press, 2006.

INDEX